We Came Through
ELLIS ISLAND

The Immigrant Adventures of Emma Markowitz

Gare Thompson

PICTURE CREDITS
Cover, pages 6–7, 11 (inset), 17 (inset), 22–25 The Granger Collection, NY; cover (inset), pages 1, 30–37 Brown Brothers, Sterling, PA; pages 2–3, 8–13, 19, 32 (top) Culver Pictures, NY; pages 4–5, 16–18, 26–27 Library of Congress; page 6 (clockwise from left) The Granger Collection, NY, Brown Brothers, Sterling, PA (3), Culver Pictures, NY; pages 14–15, 20–21, 28–29, 38–39 © Museum of the City of New York.

Library of Congress Cataloging-in-Publication Data
Thompson, Gare.
  We came through Ellis Island: the immigrant adventures of Emma Markowitz / by Gare Thompson.
      p. cm. (I Am American)
Summary: Follows a Jewish family as they leave Russia in 1893 and begin a new life in New York City, where they find new challenges and opportunities on their way to becoming Americans.
  ISBN 0-7922-5682-4 (pbk.)
  1. Marks family—Juvenile literature. 2. Marks family—Diaries—Juvenile literature. 3. Marks, Emma, b. 1881?—Family—Juvenile literature. 4. Jews—New York (State)—New York—Biography—Juvenile literature. 5. Immigrants—New York (State)—New York—Biography—Juvenile literature. 6. New York (N.Y.)—Biography—Juvenile literature. 7. New York (N.Y.)—Ethnic relations—Juvenile literature. [1. Marks family. 2. Marks, Emma, b. 1881?—Family. 3. Jews—New York (State)—New York—Biography. 4. Russian Americans. 5. Immigrants—New York (State). 6. New York (N.Y.)—History—1865–1898.] I. Title.II. Series

F128.9.J5T45 2003
974.7'1004924047'0922—dc21
[B]   2002044936

Produced through the worldwide resources of the National Geographic Society, John M. Fahey, Jr., President and Chief Executive Officer; Gilbert M. Grosvenor, Chairman of the Board; Nina D. Hoffman, Executive Vice President and President, Books and Education Publishing; Ericka Markman, President, Children's Books and Education Publishing Group; Steve Mico, Vice President Education Publishing Group, Editorial Director; Marianne Hiland, Editorial Manager; Anita Schwartz, Project Editor; Tara Peterson, Editorial Assistant; Jim Hiscott, Design Manager; Linda McKnight, Art Director; Diana Bourdrez, Anne Whittle, Photo Research; Matt Wascavage, Manager of Publishing Services; Sean Philpotts, Production Coordinator; Jane Ponton, Production Artist.

Production: Clifton M. Brown III, Manufacturing and Quality Control

PROGRAM DEVELOPMENT
Gare Thompson Associates, Inc.

BOOK DESIGN
Herman Adler Design

2004   PEN   18.00

Published by the National Geographic Society
1145 17th Street, N.W.
Washington, D.C. 20036-4688

Printed in Spain

Table of Contents

Life in Russia

From the 1880s until the 1920s, over two million Jewish **immigrants** came to the United States. Many immigrants came from Russia. In 1881 the **czar,** or ruler, of Russia was killed. Many people said that Jews had taken part in his killing. The czar's son, the new ruler, passed laws against the Jewish people. Most Jews were forced to live in the Pale of Settlement. This settlement stretched from the Baltic Sea to the Black Sea.

Life in the Pale was very hard. There were few ways to earn a living. Almost everyone was poor. Even worse were the **pogroms.** The pogroms were mob attacks on Jewish people. The Russian government encouraged these attacks. Soldiers and others destroyed stores and homes and attacked people. No one was safe. Jews could not leave the Pale without permission.

To escape their harsh life, many Jewish people decided to come to America. They often left at night. They made their way to a seaport, such as Hamburg, Germany, or Odessa, Russia. Then, with help from Jewish organizations, they bought tickets on ships sailing to the United States. Most traveled in **steerage,** the cheapest section of the ship. The journey was difficult, but the immigrants knew their lives would be better in America. And so they came.

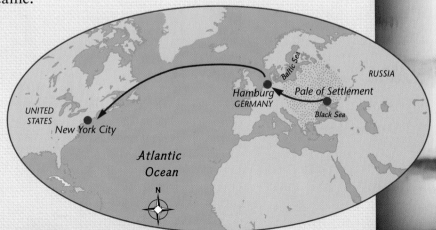

MEET THE MARKS FAMILY

In 1893 the Markowitz family decides to leave Russia. Life in the Pale is hard and dangerous. This is the story of their journey from the Pale of Settlement in Russia to the Lower East Side in New York. Their diaries and letters tell about their difficult trip and their new life in America. They also tell how the Markowitz family become the American Marks family.

Jacob Marks, father

Sofia Marks, mother

Sasha Marks, 16

Emma Marks, 12

Nathan Marks, 9

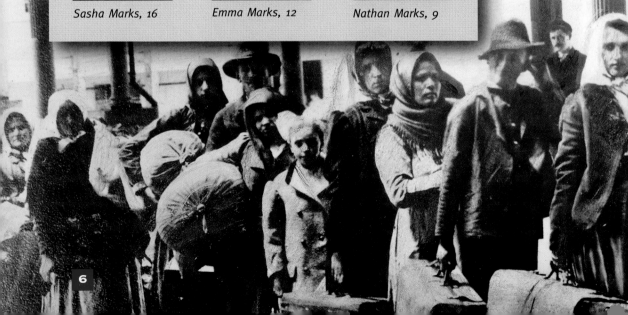

CHAPTER 1

Fleeing Russia

By 1893 more and more Jewish families in Russia were forced to move to the Pale. Once in the Pale, families struggled to earn a living. Food was scarce. Living conditions were poor. Some families were able to get out of the Pale and escape to America. From America, they wrote about getting jobs, finding homes, and feeling free.

Jacob Markowitz decided that his family had to escape, too. His son, Sasha, was 16. So far Sasha had avoided the army by going to school. Now he would have to join the Russian army for 25 years. Jacob did not have enough money to **bribe**, or pay, the Russian officials to let Sasha stay in school.

The Russian Cossacks, or soldiers, had wrecked Sofia's parents' store. The pogroms were coming more often. It seemed as though a new law was passed every day that hurt them. Jacob and Sofia plotted their escape. The family would save money for a guide. The guide would help them to escape and travel to Hamburg, Germany. Hopefully, they would not be stopped along the way. If they were stopped, it would mean prison or heavy fines.

Emma Markowitz

May 12, 1893

Father and Mother talked to us. We are leaving the Pale for America. I am scared and excited. Every day here seems worse. Soldiers are everywhere. Schools keep closing. Sometimes, I am frightened just to go to town. They say America is a land of opportunity. I do not believe, like others, that the streets are made of gold. But we would be free there.

Father says that I will have to work in America. I will also go to school. I will have to learn English. Nathan laughs when I talk about school. He says he doesn't miss it. He and his friends play in the forest all day. I read.

Father has made us all coats. Mine is not very pretty, but it is warm. Mother has sewn two gold pieces in her coat. It is most of our money. Father says the trip will cost a lot. We have to pay a guide to help us cross the Pale border. I hope we make it. I will miss my Bubbe. Who will laugh at her jokes? Not Grandfather. He is too serious, always reading.

Children selling strawberries at a rail station in Russia

Sasha Markowitz

May 13, 1893

We are leaving. I will not have to go into the army. My friend, Max, had to sign up. We have not heard from him. Our neighbor, David Cohen, finally returned. He was in the army 25 years! He looks so old, but he is only 41. He said the army is horrible. He had to eat pork. It is against our religion to eat pork. The army has no good jobs for us. David thought that he could live outside the Pale. But there is a new law. He could not live in the city of Kiev. Now, he does not work. He just sits and stares. We try to help him, but we cannot do much for him.

Helping Father repair Grandfather's store passes the time. We were lucky that the mob just destroyed the store. No one was killed. Other days, we do odd jobs. We are paid with vegetables. Father has hired a guide, Victor.

Jacob Markowitz

May 14, 1893

I have no work. There are four other tailors in the village. Only one of us has work. I can find work in America. Even Sofia can work there. I don't want to leave her parents, but we don't have the money for them to make the journey. I hope they will be safe here. We will send for them. Our guide Victor will take us over the border. I hope that we can trust him. Others have been left in the forest.

Emma Markowitz

May 20, 1893

We leave tonight. Victor will get us when it is dark. Poor Bubbe has cried most of the day. She wants mother to take her gold necklace. We can sell it in Hamburg to pay for our tickets. Mother takes it. She promises to buy Bubbe a new one.

Jacob Markowitz

May 20, 1893

I sold our tea set and Sasha's books. I told our neighbors we no longer needed them. We paid Victor his money. He will guide us to the border of the Pale. Then we follow the roads to Hamburg. He gave us names of people who will help us. Sasha and I finished building a porch today. It was our last job. The shopkeeper, Mr. Rivkin, asked us to work for him next week. We said yes. This time he paid us in cash. Does he know?

Sasha Markowitz

May 21, 1893

We left in the night. Luckily there was a moon. We traveled across the fields. Victor had hidden a wagon for us to use. We pretended we were a family of peddlers, going from village to village. Nathan says maybe in America he will be an actor. I just hope we make it to the border. I do not want to go to prison.

Harbor in Hamburg, Germany

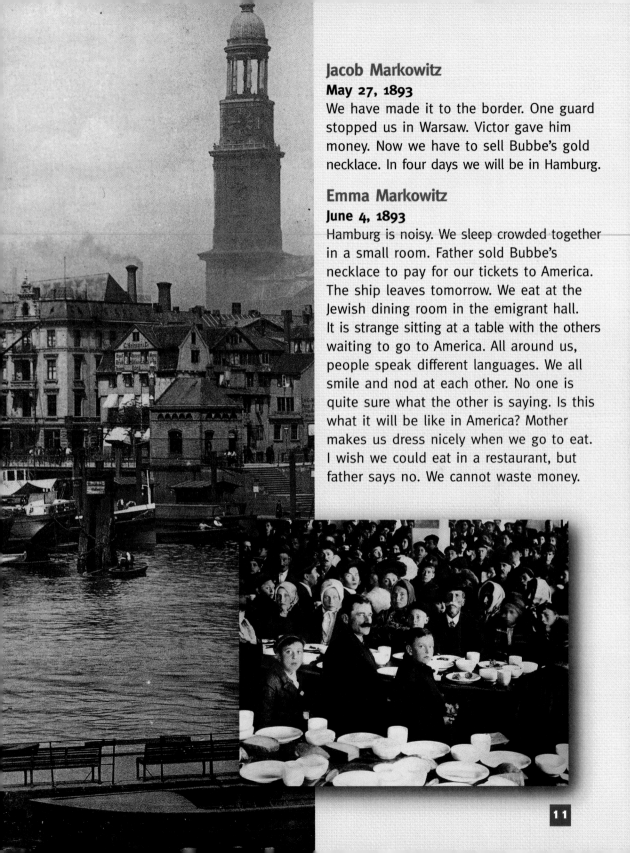

Jacob Markowitz
May 27, 1893
We have made it to the border. One guard stopped us in Warsaw. Victor gave him money. Now we have to sell Bubbe's gold necklace. In four days we will be in Hamburg.

Emma Markowitz
June 4, 1893
Hamburg is noisy. We sleep crowded together in a small room. Father sold Bubbe's necklace to pay for our tickets to America. The ship leaves tomorrow. We eat at the Jewish dining room in the emigrant hall. It is strange sitting at a table with the others waiting to go to America. All around us, people speak different languages. We all smile and nod at each other. No one is quite sure what the other is saying. Is this what it will be like in America? Mother makes us dress nicely when we go to eat. I wish we could eat in a restaurant, but father says no. We cannot waste money.

Hamburg, Germany, was a major port for the immigrants from Russia. Upon reaching Hamburg, they bought their tickets. Some of the immigrants arrived without money. Others had been cheated out of their money. They had paid for tickets that were not there. Many of the immigrants were helped by Jewish charity organizations. These organizations made sure the immigrants had tickets.

Often, the immigrants were women and children. Their husbands and fathers in America had sent for them. Others were single men hoping to make it in America. Many were tailors, grocers, or butchers.

The Markowitz family joined the other immigrants leaving for America. In America, they hoped to find a good life, too.

CHAPTER 2

Crossing the Atlantic

Russian Jews continued to stream into Hamburg. They barely had enough money for their boat tickets. Most had to travel steerage. The voyage took from one to two weeks. Hundreds of people were crammed into a very small space. Those who brought kosher food ran out of food quickly. They lived on bread, hard cheese, and tea. Families shared what little they had.

In the crowded space, disease spread rapidly. Some died on the journey. They were buried at sea. People looked forward to the few hours each day that they spent on deck in the fresh air. America seemed far away.

June 7, 1893
S.S. Nightingale

Dear Bubbe and Grandfather,

I am writing to you from our ship! We made it. We can give letters to an officer to mail. I have not been sick. Sasha and Nathan have been ill. We have run out of the food we bought in Hamburg. Now all we have is stale bread and hard cheese.

Before we boarded the ship, an officer of the ship examined us. He checked for lice. They cut my hair. Don't worry, Bubbe, it will grow back. We all passed the exam.

At night, it is hard to sleep. There are so many people crowded into the bottom of the ship. And the ship rocks so much. At first I was afraid each time we hit a wave, but now I'm not. I met a girl from Poland. She speaks some Russian. We love walking on the deck in the fresh air. In steerage, it always smells so bad.

I miss you and Grandfather.

Your loving granddaughter,
Emma

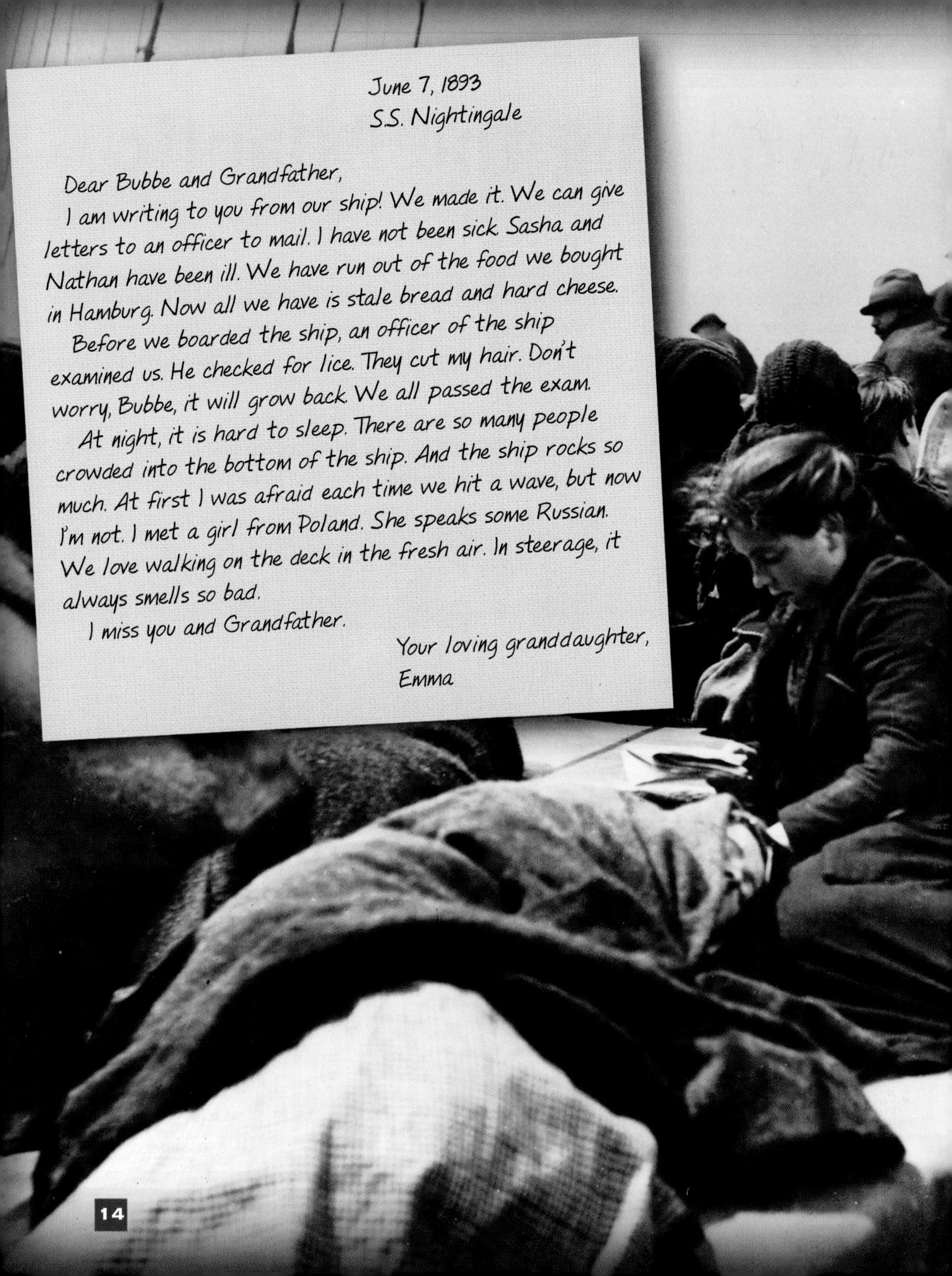

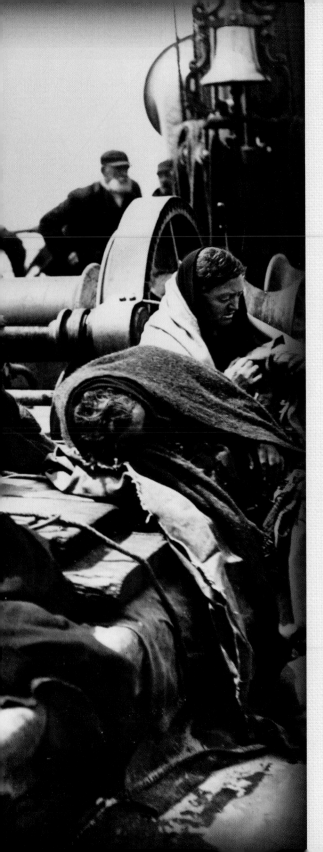

Sasha Markowitz
June 8, 1893

I hate this ship. It smells awful. This is worse than the army, but it is only for one week. Emma has not been sick. I have been sick almost every day. I spend all my time sleeping or throwing up. It is so crowded I sleep standing up. I can't sleep at night, so I count the bugs crawling up the wall. I want to scratch all the time. I think we will never get there.

Emma Markowitz
June 9, 1893

My friend Pauline's sister died last night. It was so sad. There was nothing we could do. Pauline's mother just held her. Today her parents buried her. It was horrible. They tied her body in a sheet. Then they put her overboard into the water. We said prayers, but it was not the same. Poor Pauline. All she does now is cry. I hope she does not get sick. Mother is worried about Nathan. His eyes are red and puffy.

Sasha Markowitz
June 10, 1893

At last, one day without being sick! Nathan is a little better, too. Only one eye now looks strange. I call him Cyclops, the one-eyed monster. We are allowed on the deck for short periods of time. The other people stare at us. I think I look like a scarecrow. Even the birds do not come near me. I want a bath and good food.

June 13, 1893
S.S. Nightingale

Dear Bubbe and Grandfather,
We are almost there. I am on deck. It is sunny. That is a good sign. In the distance we can see a statue. It is tall. It looks like a lady with a torch. She is wearing a crown, too. I think I hear her calling us. It is just the birds. But she is an amazing sight.

When the ship docks, we will have to go to Ellis Island. There doctors will check us. We are worried about Nathan. One of his eyes is still pink. If he is sick, will Mother have to go back with him?

A man noticed Father's coat. He asked if Father was a tailor. The man said that being a tailor is a good job. Father can make lots of money. The man's cousin has three people who work for him! He must live in a fine house and be rich. I am learning English. "How do you do?"

Your loving granddaughter,
Emma

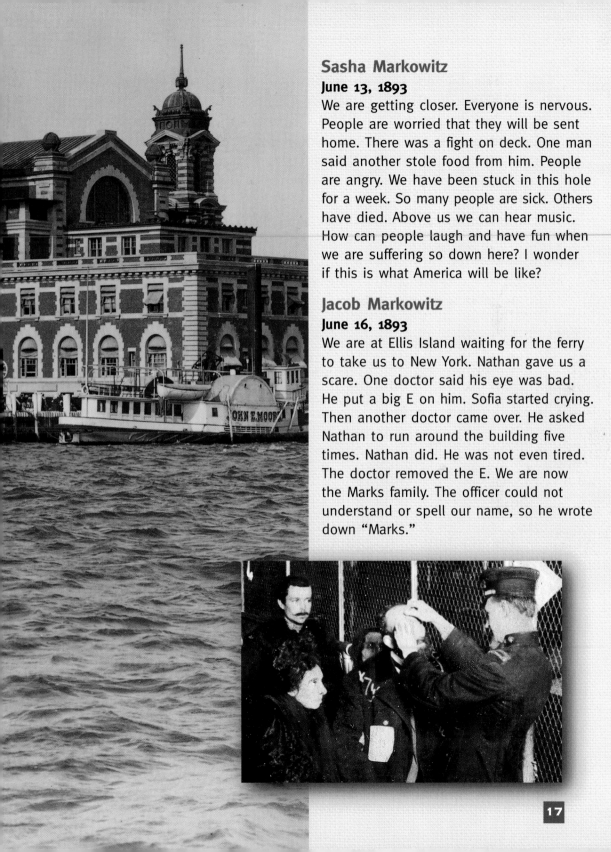

Sasha Markowitz

June 13, 1893

We are getting closer. Everyone is nervous. People are worried that they will be sent home. There was a fight on deck. One man said another stole food from him. People are angry. We have been stuck in this hole for a week. So many people are sick. Others have died. Above us we can hear music. How can people laugh and have fun when we are suffering so down here? I wonder if this is what America will be like?

Jacob Markowitz

June 16, 1893

We are at Ellis Island waiting for the ferry to take us to New York. Nathan gave us a scare. One doctor said his eye was bad. He put a big E on him. Sofia started crying. Then another doctor came over. He asked Nathan to run around the building five times. Nathan did. He was not even tired. The doctor removed the E. We are now the Marks family. The officer could not understand or spell our name, so he wrote down "Marks."

At last the immigrants were in America. They arrived at Ellis Island. There they were inspected. They were given a medical exam. They were tested for eye disease, heart problems, mental defects, or lameness. Most immigrants were worried about eye diseases. About two out of every hundred people were sent back. Sometimes whole families went back because a child did not pass. Other times, just a parent went back. Most tried to return later.

The final test was to answer questions, such as "Married? Name? Occupation?" Since many of the immigrants did not speak English, family names were often changed. Examiners wrote down what they heard or how they thought a name was spelled. But the tests didn't matter to most immigrants. They had arrived in America at last.

CHAPTER 3

Life on the Lower East Side

The immigrants took the ferry to New York City. In New York City, most immigrants went to the Lower East Side. There, they lived in **tenements,** old and rundown buildings divided into small, dark rooms. Families crowded into one or two rooms, sharing a bathroom with several other families.

For many newcomers, the Lower East Side was a shock. It was noisy. It was dirty. It was filled with people speaking many different languages. Inside the tenements, you could hear the whirring of sewing machines. Many immigrants worked in the **garment,** or clothing, industry. Many worked at home. Others worked in shops, called **sweatshops**. Hours were long and working conditions were unhealthy and dangerous.

Six months passed. The Markowitz family, now the Marks, live on the Lower East Side. They found rooms in a tenement. Everyone in the family is working.

January 3, 1894
New York City

Dear Bubbe and Grandfather,

A new year here in America. Where has time gone? Our two small rooms are dark and crowded, but they are home.

Mother works in the kitchen sewing. She makes shirts. She is paid by the shirt. I help her by finishing the shirt. I cut off all the threads. We rented a sewing machine. It only stops while we eat. In the hall, you can hear all the other machines going, too. They hum and whir all day and night! The rooms are cold. The wind blows through the cracks around the windows. We must wear our coats.

Nathan delivers bread at the crack of dawn. Then we go to school. There are 40 in my class. We sit three to a desk, but I love it! Our teacher is Irish. We are learning about America. The Fourth of July is a big holiday here.

Sasha is the only one not happy. He works with father at the factory. He hates it. He is saving to go to night school. He says he does not want to work in a sweatshop.

I hope you are doing well. I love you.

Your loving granddaughter,
Emma

Jacob Marks
January 5, 1894

The factory is so hot and dirty. Yesterday, the police came to the factory. All the children had to hide in a box. We kept right on working while the police looked around. They left after talking to the boss. I think he paid them some money. I take the children to the Education Alliance for books. I learn English there.

Sasha Marks
January 6, 1894

I hate factory work. The factories are filled with sweat, steam, and noise. The only fans are in the boss's office. I am always dripping with sweat. A friend of mine, Tom Clancy, works as a "puller." He pulls people into the stores on Hester Street. Inside they usually buy something. He makes good money. But it's not for me. Even at night the streets are so noisy and crowded. I escape to the library. The books there are free, and it is quiet. It is the only place I can think.

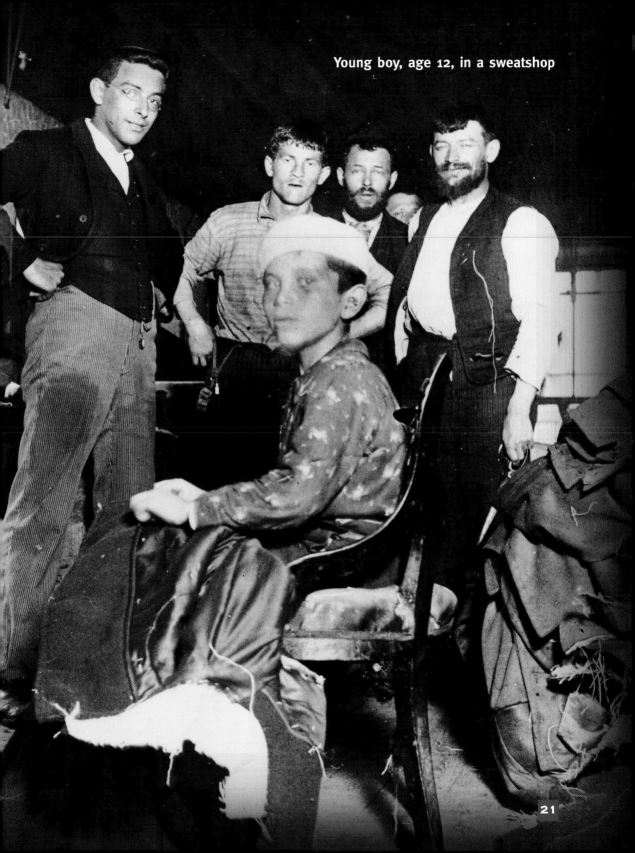

Young boy, age 12, in a sweatshop

Emma Marks

January 11, 1894

Nathan and I got new pencil boxes for school. I wanted a beautiful two-story box, but it was too much money. It was a quarter. I got a plain one for ten cents. Mother bought us some extra paper and pens. Mother wants us to do well in school. Well, at least better than Marie Simon. She lives next door to us. Her mother and my mother both sew for Mr. Golden. Mother thinks I am much smarter than Marie. I try. Poor Nathan has to go to Hebrew school, too.

Sasha Marks

January 20, 1894

Hester Street is always full of people. Peddlers sell anything you could want. The air smells of bread, pickles, and fish. Then you turn a corner and suddenly you are in Chinatown. I don't tell Mother, but I like Chinese food. I try to eat just vegetables, but there are delicious dishes with pork. The Italians on the next block sell pasta and wonderful pastries. While we go to synagogue on Friday night and quietly say our prayers, others have loud parties. I wonder what their parties are like? My friend Tom goes to them.

Jacob Marks

January 25, 1894

I am worried about Sasha. He wants so much to be American. He hates factory work. He talks about unions all the time now. If we strike, then we will lose our jobs. I do not know what to do. There is a sign on the factory door. It says, "If you don't come in on Sunday, don't come in on Monday." All we do is work. Poor Sofia's fingers are red from sewing.

Playground in a tenement alley

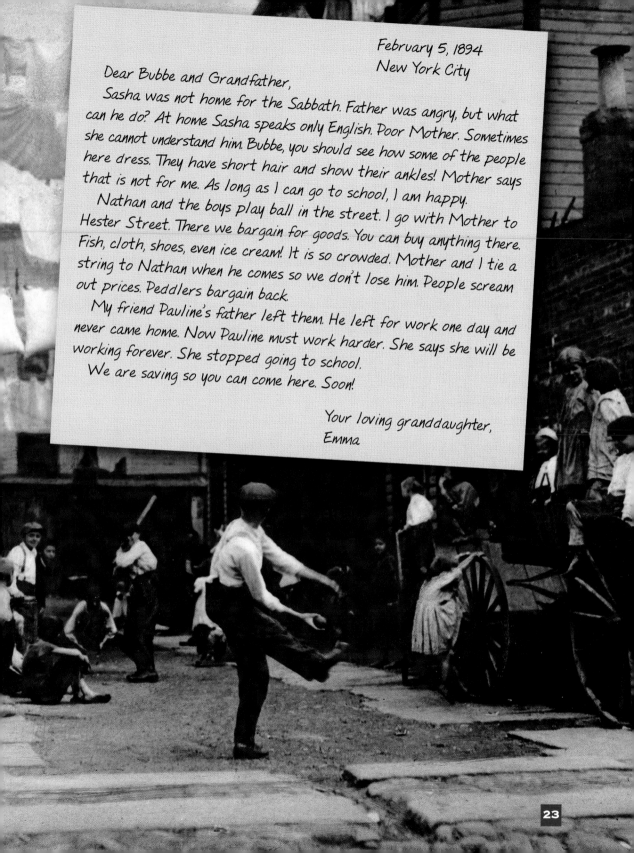

February 5, 1894
New York City

Dear Bubbe and Grandfather,

Sasha was not home for the Sabbath. Father was angry, but what can he do? At home Sasha speaks only English. Poor Mother. Sometimes she cannot understand him. Bubbe, you should see how some of the people here dress. They have short hair and show their ankles! Mother says that is not for me. As long as I can go to school, I am happy.

Nathan and the boys play ball in the street. I go with Mother to Hester Street. There we bargain for goods. You can buy anything there. Fish, cloth, shoes, even ice cream! It is so crowded. Mother and I tie a string to Nathan when he comes so we don't lose him. People scream out prices. Peddlers bargain back.

My friend Pauline's father left them. He left for work one day and never came home. Now Pauline must work harder. She says she will be working forever. She stopped going to school.

We are saving so you can come here. Soon!

Your loving granddaughter,
Emma

In 1885 there were over 200 garment factories in New York City. Most were on the Lower East Side. Factory work was hard. Conditions were dangerous. Many workers were injured on the job. There were no safety rules.

Over time, workers formed **unions**. Unions tried to help the workers. They tried to get them more money for their work. They tried to make the workplace safer. The United Hebrew Trades was formed in 1888 to help Jewish workers.

The Marks family continued to work in the garment industry. They saved their money. They sent their children to school. They still dreamed of a better life. Slowly they became more American. Sofia and Jacob spoke English as much as they did Yiddish. Emma and Nathan spoke only English. They kept many of their **traditions** from Russia, but they also learned American ways.

Becoming American

The immigrants learned to **adapt,** or change, to fit in their new country. Many learned to speak English. Others learned American ways of doing things. Many immigrants took advantage of the free libraries and schools. They wanted their children to succeed.

Two years in America had passed. The Marks family adapted. They also kept many of their traditions. They kept **kosher,** observed the Sabbath, and celebrated the Jewish holidays. Emma and Nathan had friends who were not Jewish. They played American games. They celebrated American holidays, too.

April 16, 1896
New York City

Dear Bubbe and Grandfather,

Another year here in America. I hardly remember what our old village looks like. I am sorry that Grandfather's store was attacked again. You have to come here. You are not safe there.

Mother and Father have saved and saved. We will be able to rent a larger apartment soon. There will be room for you.

Next week is Passover. We have been cleaning for over a week. We have new dishes, too. Nathan is studying with the rabbi. He will be 13 soon. It is hard to believe he will be a man. His Bar Mitzvah will be soon. He is learning Hebrew so he can read the Torah.

Sasha will be here for Passover. He lives by himself now. He is working for a union. The workers are getting ready to strike. At night, he studies law. He will become a union lawyer.

I am taking cooking classes at the Educational Alliance. I want to go to City College, but just in case, I can be a cook. Mother asks why should she do all the cooking. I'm not very good, but I will get better.

Your loving granddaughter,
Emma

Jacob Marks
April 27, 1896
We had much to be thankful for at Passover. Sasha was with us. He said prayers and gave thanks. Sofia and Emma are still sewing. Nathan is almost a man. He has three jobs. Selling newspapers is his favorite. I have been very lucky. I met Isidor Straus. He was president of the Educational Alliance. He and his brother own the large department store, Macy's. He asked me to work for him. I will sell men's clothes. No more factory work for me. It is a wonderful thing. Sofia is proud.

Emma Marks
May 2, 1896
All Nathan talks about is his Bar Mitzvah. Next year, I go to high school. Most girls stop school then. Father has said I can go!

Emma Marks
May 15, 1896

I took tests for high school. I did very well. Mother was proud. I did better than Marie, our neighbor's child. She is not going to high school. She is going to work. Her mother says she will get married first. I hope she does. I want to go to college, not get married. Yesterday I was combing Mother's hair. It is so thick and beautiful. I told her to wear it down. When I came home, she had her hair down. Not hidden in a scarf! She had the scarf around her neck. She is beautiful! She looks like a real American.

Sasha Marks
May 27, 1896

Yesterday the Board of Health, Police, and Fire Department were all on Hester Street. The made all the peddlers move their pushcarts. Some locked their carts and claimed they couldn't move. The police said they would be arrested! Finally, everyone moved. Then they cleaned the street. Gone were the smells of fish and bread. Today, everyone was back. So were the smells.

Emma Marks
June 2, 1896

We are going to the theater! It is a Yiddish play. It stars Jacob and Sarah Adler. They are famous actors! I can't wait. I hope that I can still understand enough Yiddish. I am wearing my best clothes. Mother has mentioned several times that the boy from down the hall is going, too. I just laugh. He is nice, but I am going to college. I am not getting married.

Emma Marks
June 8, 1896
Nathan sells *The Jewish Daily Forward*.
We love that paper. It is in Yiddish.
It tells you everything that is happening.
The other paper we read is the *New York Times*. It is owned by Adolph S. Ochs.
He says that his paper has "All the News That's Fit to Print." It is a good paper. He tells stories about the workers here.

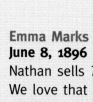

June 12, 1896
New York City

Dear Bubbe and Grandfather,
Sasha's strike is over. The workers got more money. I am happy for him. He and father still argue. Nathan is trying to be more American, too. Poor Father. Both his sons think he is too old-fashioned. To me, he is just Father.

Nathan is still loud. Now he practices his Hebrew. He is driving me crazy. I will be glad when he goes to summer camp. I told Nathan that he will be scared of the animals in the night. He laughs and says he will be fine. He goes soon.

Mother is looking at larger apartments. She thinks she found one in Harlem. That is by 125th Street. It is far from where we are now. Of course, Father has to agree, but you know Mother. Once her mind is made up, we just have to go along with her!

Your loving granddaughter,
Emma

As time passed, the immigrants did many of the same things that other Americans did. The immigrants became more social. They went to the theater. They saw plays in Yiddish theaters that told about life in the old country. They also saw plays on Broadway about American life. Theaters were places where **matchmakers** arranged for single men and women to meet. The immigrants began to do more than just work. They began to plan their futures.

A scene from a show at the Yiddish theater

Many immigrants found new and better jobs. Some opened up shops. Others went to night school. They became teachers or lawyers. Still others went to medical school to become doctors.

As they became successful, the immigrants left the tenements. They moved to places like Harlem, the Bronx, and Brooklyn. For many, the Lower East Side would always be home. They still shopped there. They went out to eat there. Their clubs were there. Like others, the Marks family moved away from the Lower East Side, but they returned often.

CHAPTER 5

Living the American Dream

As the Jewish people became more successful, some people resented their success. **Anti-semitism,** or dislike of Jewish people, grew.

Some Jewish people found that they could not stay at certain hotels. Others found that they could not live just anywhere. They had to live where Jewish people were allowed. Jewish people were not allowed to join certain clubs or organizations. However, Jewish people continued to succeed. The Marks family was becoming successful. Jacob had a good job at Macy's. Sofia no longer had to work sewing. Emma and Nathan could go to school full-time. The family moved from the Lower East Side to Harlem. To many of their friends, the Marks family was living the American Dream.

Orchard Street on the Lower East Side

September 5, 1897
Harlem, New York

Dear Bubbe and Grandfather,

We all missed you at Nathan's Bar Mitzvah. You would have been proud of him. For once, his loud voice was wonderful. He read from the Torah perfectly. Father was so proud. Mother was happy we were in the new apartment. It has four rooms! We had the dining area all set up. Father's friends from work came. It was wonderful. Of course, everyone commented on his voice. He has decided to become an actor! I promised not to tell Mother.

I go to a new school. It is two blocks from our apartment. I walk there. Many different students go there. It is not like the old school. Few speak Yiddish.

Mother asks me about different boys. I meet them at the theater. Some are nice. I still want to go to college. Sasha is now a lawyer! He opened a small office right on Orchard Street. Mother says he spends too much time working. She wants him to get married, too!

We miss you.

Your loving granddaughter,
Emma

P.S. Sasha is seeing someone! Her name is Carrie!

Emma Marks
September 9, 1897
Nathan said the kids in his new school made fun of him. They said he has funny hair. They called him bad names. I told him to ignore them. He says he misses his friends from the old neighborhood. I do, too. Nathan works after school at *The Jewish Daily Forward*. He is learning how to set type and edit. He now wants to correct my writing all the time. Mother has finally said she will think about letting me go to college. Mrs. Simon said Marie will marry a doctor. I'm not marrying!

Sasha Marks
September 11, 1897

All the talk in the cafes I go to is about the unions and our rights. The workers need a say. I hope to help them. One girl, Carrie, is joining the union. She is full of energy. Mother would not like her. She talks too much, she has strong opinions, and she is Tom's sister. I like her. We tried to get in a restaurant uptown, but we were turned away. I think it was because of me. Carrie laughed. She said the food was probably bad anyway.

Emma Marks
September 12, 1897

Father said that Bubbe and Grandfather will come here. He and Mother have sent them money. Nathan and I will sleep in the living room. It will be fine. I will still be able to read late at night. At last, I will be able to laugh at Bubbe's jokes. I will take her to the theater. She will love the plays here. Mother bought a beautiful gold necklace for her.

Jacob Marks
September 14, 1897

I saw a sign that said "No Jews." It was in an apartment building three blocks from where we live. Mr. Straus said that a friend of his was turned away from a hotel. His friend had been going there for years. America is not like the Pale. But it makes me sad. Why do people hate others? I wonder how Bubbe and Grandfather will like it here. It is a different country. Not all things are good, but many are.

September 15, 1897
Harlem, New York

Dear Bubbe and Grandfather,

I will put this letter under your plate. You will be here for Rosh Hashanah. What a perfect way to start our New Year. Mother is cooking a feast. I hope you are hungry! I made the honey cakes. I know they are your favorite. They are not as good as yours, but now you can teach me.

Sasha will be here, too. He is bringing a friend. She is a girl named Carrie. Mother keeps asking me about her. I just smile a lot. Poor Carrie. I hope she likes to answer questions.

Nathan has grown. You will see how tall he is. At last his loud voice fits his body. He still wants to be an actor. Maybe you can tell Mother that acting is a fine profession. There is a program for younger actors. Nathan applied. I hope he gets in.

My news is that I will go to college. Mother says I will be old when I marry. I don't care. I want to learn. I can't wait to tell Grandfather about the colleges here. Here we can go to school. In America we are free.

I count the days until you are here.

Your loving granddaughter,
Emma

Epilogue

The Marks family continued to succeed. Jacob worked at Macy's until he retired. He became a vice president. Sofia became active in several Jewish women's organizations. She was honored for her many contributions.

Emma did go to college. She went to City College. She was one of the few women in her class. Many dropped out to marry. Emma kept going. She became a college professor. She was one of the first woman history professors in New York. She did marry. It made her mother happy.

Sasha married Carrie and moved to Chicago. Sasha worked with the unions. He fought for the workers to win as many rights as possible. He and Emma still wrote to each other.

Nathan became an actor. Later, he worked in the Catskills as a comic. He told many of Bubbe's jokes. He worked on radio, too. Many people admired his wonderful voice.

The Marks family still came back to the Lower East Side. They visited their friends. They ate many of their meals on Hester Street. The neighborhood changed, but it was still home.

City College in New York

Glossary

adapt - to change to fit into a new situation

anti-Semitism - dislike of Jewish people

bribe - to offer someone money or a gift to persuade the person to do something for you

czar - one of the male rulers of Russia

garment - clothing

immigrant - a person who comes to live in a country in which he or she was not born

kosher - prepared according to Jewish laws

matchmaker - one who arranges or tries to arrange marriages

pogrom - mob attack on Jewish people

steerage - cheapest section of a passenger ship

sweatshop - a factory in which employees work long hours at low pay under poor conditions

tenement - a run-down apartment building in a crowded and poor part of a city

traditions - customs, ideas, or beliefs that are passed down from parents to their children

union - a group of workers joined together to improve their working conditions and pay